STAYING FRESH

Keys to Longevity in Life and Ministry

How to Avoid Burnout, Marital and Family Problems, Health Issues and Loss of Spiritual Vision

DR. KATHLEEN STEELE TOLLESON

Unless otherwise noted, all Scripture quotations are from the New King James Version of the Bible, copyright © 1979, 1980, 1982, by Thomas Nelson, Inc., Nashville, Tennessee. Portions marked "KJV" are from the Authorized King James Version of the Bible.

RECOMMENDED BY…

To all those who wish to order their lives in a more healthy way, I cannot recommend *Staying Fresh* more highly. I can promise that attending to the principles Kathy directs us to will have lasting results and that will allow us to end well.

I have known Kathy Tolleson for almost 25 years and can attest to the fact that she has always endeavored to live out the wise and practical tenets she prescribes in this book. I only wish that they had been taught to me 40 years ago when I was busy failing in nearly every area she addresses.

- *Dr. Jim Davis*

Kathy has a skill and anointing to bring prophetic, spiritual truth, coupled with wisdom and real practical application in every area of life for the believer and the ministry leader. Go To Nations is grateful to Rodney and Kathy for their countless hours ministering to GTN missionaries. *Staying Fresh* is a must read for every ministry leader and an excellent resource for keeping us properly aligned.

We all get distracted and caught up in life and work and miss the mark from time to time. I thank God for a strong mother in the faith that has gone before us and is leading the way in righteousness, peace and health, laying a proper understanding for how we not only "do" life well but really enjoy ourselves and our families in the journey.

- *Nancy Lovelace, VP of Ministries*
  Go To Nations

Staying Fresh, is must read for everyone. In today's hurry up world, it is so important to be able to stop and rest. We have to know that we are part of the Body of Christ and there are many parts, with each part having its own job to do. We are not to do it all; we need to work together and take time for refreshing and restoration. We must have our priorities in order along with good healthy boundaries to be able to make it to the end.

This is a book that is not just a one-time read; it's one that should be read a few times a year to help to keep on track so we can finish our race. Kathy has put on paper a practical teaching that can be easily followed.

- Apostle Arlene Smith
  A Call To Salvation in Jefferson, GA

FOREWORD

The world we live in is becoming more stressful and demanding every year. Financial difficulties, family breakdowns, drug and alcohol abuse and the abandonment of all moral absolutes has torn our modern world apart. For this reason it is essential that those who know they are called to love and minister to a lost and dying world maintain their own spiritual, physical and social wellbeing. Dr. Kathleen Steele Tolleson's book, Staying Fresh, provides a loving guide to maintaining the health of the fundamental elements of your life as you pour it out for the benefit of others. Staying Fresh will give you the wisdom you need to keep your balance and joy in an unbalanced and difficult world.

I love the title that she has given this book, *Staying Fresh*. It is important that those of us in ministry stay in an intimate relationship with God and not allow the things of this world to get us down, especially in relationships.

I would encourage you to read this book more than once and let God minister to you through this book.

I have been in ministry for 40 years and I have personally experienced many of the hurdles Kathleen discusses in this book. I assure you that if you prayerfully apply these principles to your own life and work, God the Father will keep you strong and fresh no matter what you encounter along life's way. He can and will "keep that which you have given Him until that day." (II Timothy 1:12) The Scriptures teach us to "be as wise as serpents and innocent as doves," and *Staying Fresh* will help you achieve all that He has commissioned you to do.

Joan Hunter
Author/Evangelist

Joan Hunter Ministries
P O Box 111
Tomball, TX 77377

281-789-7500

Go to the ministry website for all the latest in where Joan is going and what is happening at 4 Corners Conference Center

www.JoanHunter.org

DEDICATION

I am dedicating this book to all of the counselors, teachers, pastors, missionaries, caregivers and rehab who continue to lay down their lives every day to help others. Many times you are underpaid, overworked and not fully appreciated even by the people you are helping. You are the bearers of hope, the paths of freedom and builders of the future. Without you the world would have no one's hand to hold as they are led out of despair, trauma, poverty, addictions, ignorance and bondage. You are lights in the darkness and love in action. Today I thank you and I hope as you read this book and share it with others that you will be able to shine a little bit brighter for a whole lot longer.

CONTENTS

Chapter 1
An Inside Look

I originally shared the core of this message on a mountain top with a group of educators from San Pedro Sula, Honduras. At the time, the city they worked and lived in was the murder capital of the world. The children they taught came from such extremely poor areas that some of them did not know how to use a toilet. They had to be educated on how to use a bathroom facility. Those teachers and administrators had a heart to make a difference in the children, their city and their nation. They were surrounded by stressful conditions.

I have had the opportunity to see similar sights in an orphanage and school in Uganda, in a tribal pastor's retreat in the Philippines, ministering to a pastor and his family in Nepal and in other places I have visited throughout the world. America is filled with people dedicated to helping others not only in their own country but throughout the world.

In my introduction that evening, I shared how I had been in some sort of helping profession or capacity for forty years yet I still had excitement and energy for what I was doing. My marriage was prospering and my health was better than it had been in years. I wanted them to understand that even though difficult, it was possible. And I wanted to help them understand what I had to learn the hard way and also the lessons I had learned from the lives of others.

As I completed my message, I felt a nudging from the Lord that it was something I was to share with others and that my outline was the beginning of a book. I kept the title of the book the same as the message that evening, *Staying Fresh.* Many of the things I will be sharing you may already know, but it always helps to reinforce and remind us what we need to be doing.

Unnecessary Prices

Over the years, I have worked in special programs for children, counseled, pastored, consulted and have been involved in short-term missions. I've had the opportunity to meet, co-labor with and lead many dedicated, wonderful people. I have also had the opportunity of knowing and ministering to people who have paid unnecessary prices with their health, longevity, marriages and families.

I can't tell you how many families I have counseled who sacrificed their children on the altar of ministry. What do I mean by that? I am talking about the children who never really have their mom or dad's full attention because they are always too busy ministering to or taking care of someone else. When they aren't, they are too tired to do anything for their own family. They sacrifice family time and vacations for everybody else. There is no time for events that create happy family memories and one day the children grow up and don't want to serve the God that robbed them of their childhood. Many times these pastors who were once helping other families find themselves needing family reconciliation. They may be visiting their prodigal son or daughter in a drug treatment facility or grieving the loss of relationship. It's an unnecessary price. It's a price God is not asking us to pay. It's a price extracted by performance, our own ambitions and are inability to have healthy boundaries. The investment in marriage and family memories cannot be underestimated. And it doesn't always have to take a lot of time. Memories can be made in moments. I love the saying, *"Life is not measured by the number of breaths you take, but by the number of moments that take your breath away."*

I have had to grieve the loss of friends who died prematurely because they ignored warnings related to their health. They were men and women with so much to give but their lives were cut short. They were too busy to eat healthy, to exercise and to recover from an operation or an illness. They were so busy taking care of everyone else that they neglected to take care of themselves. Again, it's an unnecessary price. It robs their families, their legacies and leaves visions unfulfilled.

I have also had an inside look into too many marriages that were either in critical condition or had already moved into premature death; others had been on life-support for years. A healthy marriage requires time, energy and resources. I've spent time with ministers on the mission field who have simply become partners in the work they are doing. Their spiritual, physical and emotional intimacy has been stolen by the needs and demands of their work. They are robbed of the joy of their relationship and the strength of their union.

I've sat in a counseling room as a pastor laid hands and prayed for his wife and she broke down crying because it was the first time she experienced what thousands of other people had when he ministered to them. The minister had never ministered to his first ministry, his wife. I've seen first-hand churches, ministries and businesses collapse when the marriage of the leaders fell apart. I've also counseled those now walking alone

4

because they were too busy, too driven, to take care of their marriage, which ended in divorce. So many pastors tell themselves that divorce will never happen to them, all the while neglecting their spouse for the sake of the sheep. It is so sad to see the disillusionment and the pain and suffering that could have been avoided by understanding and living some basic principles, again a price that no one should have to pay.

I have been brought into dysfunctional ministries for a "quick fix" to problems created by a system that was unhealthy. Demands made of leaders, staff and church attendees caused the breakdown of families, unnecessary stress and an environment that opened the door to a performance based life style riddled with hidden sin. Early on, the Lord gave me a vision of His Church. He showed me a bright red shiny apple. It looked so good on the outside. Then a finger pushed into a soft spot and it was rotten to the core. Everyone wants a "quick fix" for fruit that is the result of a toxic system.

The Purpose

The purpose of *Staying Fresh* is to equip you with practical and spiritual principles that will prevent you, your family and the people you serve from being robbed. As I said earlier, some of these I learned the hard way through my own life, others

I learned from those who mentored me and some were learned through an inside look at the lives of many people in helping professions.

That night in Honduras I shared one of the first nuggets I ever received. It was a truth that I have tried to live by for the past forty years. I was a houseparent at a children's home. It was one of my first jobs helping others. I was only in my twenties but was married and had two children of my own. We had ten other teenagers in the group home we managed for five days a week, plus I was taking college classes while the older children were in school. Many of the older children had behavioral problems, so life was full of ups and downs and stress.

One of the counselors at the facility took me aside one day and gave me this piece of advice:
She said, *"Kathy, I see you have a real heart for these kids and you do a lot of extras for them. But I don't want you to get burnt out. It's okay to care and pour your heart into this place, but when it's time to be with your family and take care of yourself you need to put that as a priority. Don't take the burdens and problems home with you. Good people like you are hard to find, but if you really care you'll want to make it for the long haul and that means taking care of yourself and your family."*

It wasn't always easy but from then on I worked hard at keeping healthy boundaries. I will be sharing more on establishing and keeping healthy boundaries in Chapter 5. Have crises sometimes upset the apple cart of family and personal times? Absolutely! But I have still managed them in a way that did not consume me or take all my time. I am so thankful to have received that advice at such a young age. I really respected the woman who shared it with me and took it to heart. Many times over the years those words have rung in my ears. I hope as you read *Staying Fresh,* you're able to glean something that will help you run your race to the finish. 2 Timothy 4:7 - *I have fought the good fight, I have finished the race, I have kept the faith.*

Chapter 2
Spiritual Refreshing

Acts 3:19 states, "Repent therefore and be converted, that your sins may be blotted out, so that times of refreshing may come from the presence of the Lord." According to this Scripture, refreshing comes from His presence.

On the day I was ordained in 1991, Dr. Bill Hamon spoke a prophetic word over me. He said that even though I was going to be busy, busy, busy, God was calling me to keep the oil of His presence and anointing flowing so that the wick would not burn. I knew it was similar advice to what I had received in my twenties. The wick represented the core of my being. God did not want that to burn. If the wick burns the light or candle is extinguished. When the wick is soaked with oil; the lamp burns continually. And the oil can always be replenished. We have to learn how to work with the Lord and not just with our own strength and abilities. He can do what we can't do.

It's exciting to see the revelation of "soaking" coming to the Body of Christ. "Soaking" is simply spending time in His presence. It usually is referring to personal or corporate time of spiritual intimacy accompanied by worship music. If we as His ministers are to be flames of fire, as it states in Psalm 104:4, we have to have something that burns. We need to be soaked in the oil of the Lord, His anointing, so that we don't run out of oil. (run dry and burn out or burn up)

There is a presence of the Lord that comes when we gather together. Here's what the Bible says:

- Matthew 18:20, *"For where two or three are gathered together in my name, there am I in the midst of them."* He also inhabits the praises of His people.
- Psalms 95:2 instructs, *"Let us come before His presence with thanksgiving; Let us shout joyfully to Him with psalms."*
- Psalm 100:4 declares, *"Enter into His gates with thanksgiving, and into His courts with praise: be thankful unto him, and bless His name."*

So times of personal and corporate worship also release His Presence. I know many times I've had to fulfill ministry obligations when I wasn't feeling well. As I entered into worship, I would be empowered by the strength and anointing of God and able to preach and teach with no problem.

Other times, I would have to press in so I could minister to people personally. If I was tired or not feeling well, a good worship CD on the way to my appointment could make a difference!

Refresh - Recharge - Renew

We all need to learn what works for us. There are some times in my own life when I need alone time with the Lord. It's one of the ways I personally recharge. Just as Jesus would draw to himself on the mountain top and spend time with His Heavenly Father, I need the presence of the Lord in a personal way. I need to be quiet so I can hear His "still, small voice" 1 Kings 19:12. There is a difference in the anointing given to us to give away and the anointing that refreshes and restores us. I like to say there is an anointing for ministry and an anointing for life. Staying refreshed requires both. We need time with Him so He can trim our wicks and keep us healthy. Jesus gave us the pattern to follow; a time to minister to the people, a time to fellowship with family and those close to us and a time to be alone. Too often we wait until we're so burnt out to really draw aside and take time with Him. It's sad to watch leaders in ministry and see them attending to everything else in a service, rather than taking the time to really enter into the presence of the Lord.

I also find that nature helps refresh me. God

created it and I believe we can find Him in it. I don't believe we are called to worship the earth or its elements, but I can see His Glory in the beauty of a sunrise, His Majesty in mountain vistas and His Power in the roar of the ocean. In Romans 1:20 the Bible says, *"For since the creation of the world His invisible attributes are clearly seen, being understood by the things that are made, even His eternal power and godhead, so that they are without excuse."* In any great work of art, there is always a sense of its creator. It's one of the reasons I enjoy motorcycling, because it connects me to nature which connects me to God. In a car, you might get to smell the air freshener or maybe the new leather interior. When you ride, you can smell literally smell the flowers, the fresh cut grass, a grove of pine trees and even the rain. We talk about stopping to smell the roses. But when was the last time, you really stopped and appreciated the beauty of God's creation that surrounds you? He created it to refresh you and bless you. Stop and smell His roses.

The Bible says in 1 Corinthians 14:4, *"He who speaks in a tongue edifies himself,"* and in Jude 1:20, *"But you, beloved, building yourselves up on your most holy faith, praying in the Holy Spirit, keeping yourselves in the love of God, looking for the mercy of our Lord Jesus Christ unto eternal life."* When I start feeling weak or my love and mercy are almost on empty, I know I haven't been praying in the Spirit enough. It's a wakeup call. Praying in the Spirit is another way we stay refreshed and built up in the Lord. In John 7:37-39, Jesus shared, *"If anyone thirsts, let him come to me and drink. He who believes in Me, as the Scripture has said, out of his heart will flow rivers of living water. But this He spoke concerning the Spirit, whom those believing in Him would receive; for the Holy Spirit was not yet given because Jesus was not yet glorified."* If I am going to bring life and refreshing to others, I have to have living water flowing through me. It's like having rechargeable batteries. When they start running down you can just plug them into a higher energy source and they can receive a new charge. Praying in the Spirit helps recharge your spiritual battery. It is our own hydroelectric plant. For more on the Holy Spirit and praying in tongues I recommend Dr. Bill Hamon's book, *70 Reasons for Speaking in Tongues,* which can be found online at www.Amazon.com.

The Word is also likened to water in the Bible. One of the greatest ways in the natural to be refreshed is to hydrate ourselves. Spiritually we need to stay hydrated in the Word of God. Dehydration in the natural causes weariness, irritability and confusion. Sound familiar? If it does then maybe you're suffering from spiritual dehydration. There's a difference in being in the Word preparing a message and being in the Word to take a drink for ourselves. I can be in the kitchen and fill a pitcher of water to serve to others but it won't help me if I'm thirsty. I need my own glass of water. Without our own renewal, those that are helpers of mankind can end up bitter and resentful. They have poured themselves out and now have nothing left. It's not what God intended. He has a plan and methods to help us stay fresh. The Word even tells us in Proverbs 11:25 that the one who waters will also be watered. Other translations of the same scripture say that one who refreshes will be refreshed. We just have to partake of it and we need to know that we can't do it on our own. We need Him and we need others.

Chapter 3
Importance of Community

Fellowship with the saints refreshes. Paul shares in 1 Corinthians 16:17-18 *"I am glad about the coming of Stephanas, Fortunatus, and Achiacus for what was lacking on your part they supplied. For they refreshed my spirit and yours. Therefore acknowledge such men."* Then again in Romans 15:32 he shares, *"that I may come to you with joy by the will of God and may be refreshed together with you."* The Apostle Paul had a revelation; fellowship is a key to refreshing. It's essential to longevity of service.

There are times that we all need the comfort of fellowship. It is a comfort that refreshes us. 2 Corinthians 7:13 states, *"Therefore we have been comforted in our comfort. And we rejoice exceedingly more for the joy of Titus, because He has been refreshed by you all."* Sometimes when you travel to the nations you can experience beds that are not quite as comfortable as your own.

And that's an understatement. There is nothing like climbing back in your own bed for a refreshing night's sleep. Good fellowship is like that. It is comfortable and refreshing. When it's not, we need to examine ourselves and our relationships.

Refresher Killers

Here are some issues that can cause us <u>not</u> to be refreshed by fellowship. One of them is that we are simply fellowshipping with the wrong people. They have no life giving water to share with us. It's important to examine our relationships. Do they refresh us or drain us? There is a difference in spending time with people to serve them or to honor them and having relationship that is part of our personal recharging system. I have some relationships that I know a twenty minute phone call will refresh and energize me. As the Apostle Paul shared, we need to acknowledge such people. Then there are relationships that I know my spiritual battery must be charged because even a five minute call can be draining. We also need to look at the fellowship we provide others: is it life giving? If you're really brave, ask some family, friends and business associates to give you feedback on how often you help them recharge and refresh. It may not be what you want to hear, but feedback is important for our growth. It's important to always keep in mind that we have to sow in order to reap.

Performance is another fellowship refresher "killer." When we are in performance mode we will never be truly refreshed by spending time with others. We might be excited by spending time with someone we consider important. We may enjoy time with someone who bought into our performance, but there is a difference in truly being refreshed. Can you relax and be yourself around people when you fellowship with them? If not, you are probably dealing with performance issues or social anxiety. It's important to get ministry and deal with the issue because it stops up one of God's conduits of refreshing.

Perfectionism usually goes hand in hand with performance and robs of us our ability to receive refreshing from community. We will either be irritated and angry with ourselves or others for not living up to our expectations. Our kids might not act perfectly at the church family day or our spouse may be less than attentive. We are left frustrated and robbed of the time we could have enjoyed. Disappointment colors our relationships with others. Time spent together never really satisfies. Perfectionism is always accompanied by a critical spirit because it has to seek out that which isn't perfect and ends up focusing on that rather than what is good. It is a counterfeit to a spirit of excellence that can only be created by God. You can have excellent fellowship with very imperfect people if God's Spirit is involved. I've seen this portrayed many times in praise and worship teams. When the leader strives to be perfect, it creates performance and self-consciousness in a team. Emphasis is on developing talent and not relationship. There is no refreshing for them or the congregation even though they might play great music. When the leader allows God to anoint the worship, He makes it excellent by His presence. Emphasis is placed on each person having a relationship with the Lord, which allows intimacy with God to spill over to the congregation. Talent can still be developed, but it is in right priority and not driven by perfectionism.

Control issues also affect our ability to receive refreshing from fellowship. Instead of being able to relax and enjoy the time we spend with others, our control issues kick in and, rather than receiving, we move into control related to conversation, environment, perception, etc. It's exhausting, so we either avoid fellowship or find lukewarm fellowship that won't confront us but also won't satisfy us. Control is usually the fruit of fear and shame. In the *Restoring the Foundations Ministry* developed by Chester and Betsy Kylstra this is referred to as the *Shame, Fear, Control Cycle*. From childhood, we develop a shame based identity through generational sin, our own sin and through the sins of the people around us and then we live in fear of people discovering who we really are. It

18

is a very subconscious mechanism but when it is deactivated through ministry people find themselves free from stress and the need to be in control. Our control issues will actually repel people rather than draw the relationships we so need.

Why We Need Community

In Proverbs 18:1 says, *"A man who isolates himself seeks his own desire; He rages against all wise judgment."* We were designed and created for community. People who use their relationship with God to isolate themselves from fellow Christians and humanity are deceived. They develop a spiritual superiority that says all I need to do is spend time with God. He and I have a special relationship. When that relationship separates you from the ability to relate and fellowship with others, you've missed the boat and you've missed God's heart. If you did open- heart surgery on God, you would find His heart full of people. *"For God so loved the world,"* so if we are truly in relationship with God, we will develop His heart for people. Isolation even guised in a covering of spirituality will never keep you fresh. You will eventually be taken over by the spirit of deception because you won't have a multitude of counsel surrounding you to help keep you on a balanced path.

Ephesians 4:16 says, *"from whom the whole body, joined and knit together by what every joint supplies, according to the effective working by which every part does its share, cause growth of the body for the edifying of itself in love."* If we are an isolated part we can't do our share. We cannot supply anyone else and we also do not receive supply. It does not cause growth in the Body of Christ. In our natural bodies, cells that do not have team participation are called cancer. They actually work against the body and are not team players. They cannot receive from other cells and go off and do their own thing. Rather than submitting to divine order, they create their own kingdom. Community causes us to grow as we help grow others. It's healthy even though at some times it may be difficult because community also causes our issues to be exposed.

"As iron sharpens iron, so a man sharpens the countenance of his friend." This statement is found in Proverbs 27:17. What does it mean? Relationship with true intimacy sharpens us. It makes us better. It confronts our dull edges and the places where our life has been nicked and needs restoring. Healthy relationships cause us to be healthier people. I'm sure an axe doesn't always look forward to a good sharpening. But when it goes up against a strong tree, it's thankful for the process. We wonder why marriage can feel like a grinding of our very fiber. It's how God

designed it. If we allow the process to take place, we are better people in every area of our lives. If we fight it we simply become more self-protective and defensive. Can you imagine an axe coming to a sharpening with a blade protector on it? That's the way a lot of people handle their relationships. We have to lay down our defense mechanisms if they are going to become a place of refreshment and renewal. Recently Rodney and I celebrated our thirtieth wedding anniversary and, as we were reminiscing and sharing at dinner, I told him that I liked who I had become by being married to him. Our marriage relationship has required healing, maturity, change and walking out the fruit of the spirit in daily life. Not always easy, but always fruitful and productive.

Another Scripture that illustrates the process is, *"Faithful are the wounds of a friend."* Proverbs is full of wisdom and this tells us that in a true friendship everything isn't always peaches and cream – sweet and smooth. I like to say that the wounds of a friend are faithful to find our deeper wounds. My husband and I have been true friends; we have been faithful to expose each other's wounded areas. But it has led us to deeper healing and not rejection of the relationship. As we are transparent before the Lord and each other, we can ask the Holy Spirit why the other person's words or actions caused us to overreact or close down. Usually, it is rooted in a past experience.

Once the cause is revealed by the Holy Spirit we can forgive and ask Jesus to come and bring healing. Through the process, our spouse becomes a healing agent rather than the enemy. The relationship becomes a life giving oasis rather than a sentence of desert wandering. Yes, community and fellowship is a facet of God's plan for us to stay fresh and growing; but we have to have a revelation and allow personal ministry to take place so we can truly partake of it.

Chapter 4
Priorities

Nothing can cause problems any more quickly than misplaced priorities. As a pastor and counselor, I have gotten to see this one up close and in person. So many of the people I counsel have problems because their priorities are out of order. I use this as a priority indicator: God, Marriage, Family and Ministry/Profession in that order.

All you have to do is look at your schedule to see where your priorities lie. Usually our schedule reflects our ministry/profession before it reflects God, marriage or family. I understand that we all have work to do. But do we take time to schedule time with the Lord, our spouse and our families or do they just get the crumbs of our life? I know in the past I have been very guilty of this but have worked hard to correct it. It's not easy. Life has demands. But if we don't take a stand and carve out our priorities, life won't do it for us. It's a rare boss that will say, "You're spending too much time at work, go home and enjoy your family." And only a spiritually sensitive spouse will say, "You need to spend some time with the Lord this morning, then we can enjoy some time together later." We can't trust the world to help us keep our priorities in order.

We also have to be careful that legalism doesn't enter into how we see our priorities. If we try to give everyone equal time every day, it doesn't work. There are days it's important to spend time with our kids and other times we need to take a date night. I may shut myself up with the Lord for a day and only spend the evening with my husband. Priorities come out of a revelation of our source and what we need to be able to meet our other priorities. I have to have time with the Lord to be the person I need to be for all the other people in my life. Then I need to keep my core relationship with my husband healthy so our marriage stays intact so our family stays intact. And for me to give what it takes in ministry or at my job, I do that best when I am strengthened and secure in my relationship with the Lord, my husband and my family. Any employer will tell you that an employee with marriage and family problems isn't a productive employee. We work when our priorities work.

There is nothing sadder to see than a minister who has given their life to serving others but then loses their marriage or children because their family was never a priority. Earlier I talked about the children I have seen sacrificed on the altar of ministry. This is exactly what I was talking about, the problems that occur in families when priorities are not healthy. But what causes us to have unhealthy priorities in the first place?

Causes of Unhealthy Priorities

Here are a number of things I have observed over the years: First, some of it is just plain, old human ambition. This especially attacks young ministers or those just starting out but if it's not corrected it can continue to drive people for a lifetime. Ambition can cause us to keep working long past what the Lord is requiring of us. Pride is like a fuel additive on ambition. When you combine the two, people keep striving and striving. For God to truly use a life, he will kill ambition and human zeal, as demonstrated in the lives of so many of His servants. Some of it is human nature that must be exchanged for a Christ like nature. Others have deeper issues that come from a wounded childhood. They are still trying to prove that they can "amount to something" or that they aren't "stupid." Driven by the fear of becoming the message of their childhood, they are unable to set healthy priorities until they receive healing from the past.

A second area that I have seen cause out of order priorities is a result of avoiding issues and problems. Passivity can play a big role in this, too. Let me give you a couple of examples. If a man is having relational problems with his wife and children, it's easier to stay at work longer or spend time caretaking someone or something else. They experience more personal rewards and pats on the back for being so wonderful in other areas of their life and, before you know it, life has reinforced them to spend less time with their wife and children. A wife may begin to pour all of her time and energy into the children and home, because it feeds her picture of being the perfect mom and housewife and it's easier than working through a genuine relationship with God and her husband. In the midst of creating her fantasy life, she leaves little time for her relationship with the Lord or her spouse. One day he walks out, tiring of having a wife who won't let him discipline or have relationship with his children and a home that is a showpiece and not a place to live. Now, she's mad at God and doesn't have the income to keep her own issues at bay by constantly shopping and creating the perfect family image. These scenarios come in many packages and forms but they will all have the same thing in common: AVOIDANCE. Human nature does what's easiest. To stay fresh we have to develop a Christlike nature and work through issues in order to keep healthy priorities.

26

A third area is ignorance. Sometimes people do not know any better. They have not been taught. They have never seen healthy priorities modeled. They have never been taught how to set boundaries, a topic we will be discussing in the following chapter. Many people think their service to God is putting God first. Rather than putting their own personal spiritual relationship with God first, everything they are doing to serve Him comes first, which means burnout is right around the corner. Also, if their service is first because they are serving God, then it means that their spouse and family are standing in a very long line of other people in order to have their needs met. I hate to say this but some ministries, churches, service organizations and businesses prey on people who do not have healthy priorities. They will consume them. As leaders, it's our job to disciple people while providing them with healthy role models in the area of Godly priorities.

Another area is what I call "lost time." Lost time can be a result of many factors. I didn't get saved until I was in my thirties; I have to make up for lost time. I didn't get married until later in life; I have to make up for lost time. I haven't been financially successful yet, I have to make up for lost time. Scripturally, there is no lost time. The Bible tells us that the Lord can redeem all things. It also tells us in Romans 8:28 that we can know all things work together for good to those who love God, to those who are called according to His purpose. Until we get our theology right, we can can't our life right. As long as we are striving in some area of our life to "make up for lost time," we are at risk of having priorities that are out of order.

Family, social and financial pressures can cause us to throw our priorities to the wind. Romans 8:14 tells us that those who are led by the Spirit of God are sons of God. With so many life demands, unless we are led by the Spirit it is very difficult to juggle or meet our priorities with our own human ability. I love redeemed time. I have had a day with my husband that has felt like a week and an hour with the Lord that has felt like a day. I might have an hour at work where I accomplish what I normally would have in two days. When I am led by the Lord and not simply the demands of life, I find there is more meaning and productivity in my time. This weekend was a good example for me. It was Thanksgiving weekend and I felt led to declare it as a writers retreat for me. My husband had some obligations to fulfill and our family had celebrated a holiday meal the prior Sunday. Suddenly on Friday afternoon, I felt that we were supposed to purchase a Christmas tree for one of our daughters and her family. I called my husband, who already had a trailer hooked up to his truck (something I didn't know that made it easier). Then I called my other daughter to see if she was ready for her tree. We would pick it up and help set it up for her. I didn't realize our two daughters and their children were having a sleep-over. So in a very short time there were two families blessed and a happy grandma because I was able to see all the kids in a very short time, have a special experience with them and then get back home to continue working on *Staying Fresh.* I have a life and schedule that requires me to be led by the Spirit. When I do; it works and when I don't; the wheels of life start grinding and I know I need more oil on my priorities. In order to be led by the Spirit and deal with the demands placed on us by others, we need to have healthy boundaries. It is an important enough area that it will be discussed in its own upcoming chapter.

I have just listed a few common areas that can cause people to have out-of-order priorities. But each of us has to examine our own priorities. Are they misplaced? And if so, why? The Lord's Prayer instructs us to pray, *"Your Kingdom come on earth as it is in heaven."* A kingdom has order; it has government. As we submit to the Lord's divine order and government, life gets better. In Romans 14:17 it says that the Kingdom of God is righteousness, peace and joy in the Holy Spirit. If you're lacking in those areas, I encourage you to examine your priorities with the help of the Holy Spirit.

Chapter 5
Healthy Boundaries

Interestingly enough, as I was getting ready to write this chapter I had lunch with a young lady who works in a missionary organization. We ended up talking about some problem areas that had been cropping up in her life. As we looked at each one, they all had one thing in common, BOUNDARIES. I can't tell you how important they are for longevity in ministry and for your own sanity and well-being.

Ministers have the worst time setting boundaries. Scriptures that talk about laying down our lives and being servants make it very confusing. If we really love God and our fellow man, can we ever tell anyone "no"? I'm here to tell you, if you really love God and your fellow man, it's essential to learn how to establish boundaries. Jesus did! There were times when he went off completely alone to pray and spend time with His Father. He also set some pretty strong boundaries regarding

31

money changers in the temple. When Lazarus had died, Jesus didn't run immediately to His gravesite. He finished what He was doing and then went and raised him from the dead. Actually, God's Word is all about boundaries. When ministers do not set boundaries they end up with marriage and family problems, health issues and can suffer from burn-out. Some people think the only way to set a boundary is to put up a wall. That is really the true definition of burn-out. I no longer have the resources to be able to keep up with the demand of the ministry therefore, "I'm done!"

First let's talk about what they are and what they aren't. Boundaries can be applied in all of our relationships. Healthy personal boundaries give us the ability to allow certain things into our lives while not allowing other things into our lives. We can have physical boundaries. *"It's okay to shake my hand but it's not okay to hug me."* We can have boundaries related to our home. *"You can come and visit me if you call in advance, but if you just stop by I won't be answering the door."* Boundaries are needed related to family relationships. *"Yes, I can help you with the grandkids today, but I won't be able to tomorrow."* Boundaries are important in marriages. *"Honey, I'd love to have sex with you tonight, but right now I have to get ready for an appointment."* Work boundaries might sound something like this, *"I would be happy to finish this project for you, but I won't be able to take it home over the weekend. I'll be able to complete it by Tuesday."* From those examples, you can see that every area of our life needs boundaries.

Boundaries can be communicated non-verbally, but for the most part boundaries are best understood by others through verbal communication. Many people feel uncomfortable communicating boundaries to others because they are afraid of their reactions. It's important to communicate boundaries clearly and in advance when possible. For example, a pastor can establish boundaries with his congregation by requiring them to call and make an appointment for personal ministry. It's also healthy because a simple open door policy can cause some people to consume the majority of time while others are left out. Remember, you are not responsible for someone's reaction but you can help people better receive your boundaries by setting them with the right heart and spirit.

I would use a number code for people I counseled that needed more support than others. It helped me to set boundaries related to communication. If they called and left a message and gave it a # 1 that meant not urgent, give me a call whenever; #2 meant it's important and as soon as you are able, give me a call; and #3 was URGENT, call me right away. It is very difficult to set boundaries with wounded, hurting people for several reasons. First of all, you wouldn't be in your line of work if you didn't have compassion.

Secondly, with wounded, hurting people most actions and communication are looked at through the lenses of abandonment and rejection. Third, you always have to judge what is genuine and when it is a demand for attention. Attention is very important, because it shows them someone cares, and it is comforting but cannot be the basis for ministry.

People often flip-flop between the extremes of no boundaries and walls. They will do everything for everybody and then disappear and isolate. They will be involved in every ministry in the church and then pull out of everything and stay home and watch church on TV. Family members will not be able to say, "no." Their alternative is to pull out of relationship and you rarely see them. Sexual abuse victims tend to have huge problems with boundaries; basically, because one of the primary areas of boundaries should be to that of our own bodies. When those boundaries are violated, their "no" has been taken away. It's one of the reasons that you will find sexual abuse victims operating in opposite extremes. They will either have no boundaries and move into promiscuity even to the point of prostitution or they will have walls and be frigid and unable to enjoy the intimacy of marriage.

Some people have problems setting and

enforcing boundaries with people who are in authority over them. It's one of the reasons cults can establish extreme control over people. I always have shared with people with whom I work that I want them to be able to say no to me when needed. I can get over-excited about a project and work late or send an idea on the weekend, but they need to know it's okay to set a boundary and say, "I have to go home now." It's healthy. People who are raised in authoritarian homes may not feel they have the right to boundaries related to anyone in authority. Another problem area can arise from performance issues. To be loved and accepted, we have to do everything and do it perfectly. Fear of rejection causes many people to have serious trouble setting boundaries. "If I say, "no" will they still love me?" Other people have the fear of making someone angry. They give in and do whatever the other person wants so they don't get mad. It is not your job to be responsible for other people's emotions. If you set a healthy boundary and they get angry, then you will have to let them. Walking on eggshells is an enabling behavior. It doesn't help the person face their anger and the person enabling only ends up resentful and finally puts up a wall. Sometimes you may find it difficult to set boundaries with a certain personality type. Usually it is caused by a childhood relationship where boundaries were not allowed or created difficulty when expressed. The individual from childhood may have a similar personality to the person you are now trying to establish a boundary with and it may take some personal examination and healing first.

Because of all these emotional reasons, setting and enforcing boundaries isn't as easy as it sounds. Sometimes we have to get to personal issues, many times stemming from our childhood, to be able to discover the root of why we have difficulty setting boundaries. A mother who never allowed any privacy and always had to know all of your business could cause you not to be able to simply say to someone, "I'm not comfortable with answering that question." An angry father, who would burst into your room without knocking and had even kicked your sister's door in, could easily be the reason that you're scared to ask your partner to please knock before they barge into your office. The ability to set and enforce boundaries is a sign of maturity. It also may be helpful to share some of your past experiences to allow people to understand where the boundary is coming from. For example, "When you open the door without knocking it makes me feel unsafe. Can you please knock first?"

Whether in business or ministry, lack of boundaries and walls cause problems on team efforts. It's difficult to build a team where everyone doesn't have a concept of boundaries. Can you imagine a workplace where "no boundaries" meets "walls"? It sounds something like this. "I can't believe she just came in my office and took post it notes off of my desk." Or "He's in sales and needs to stay out of the service area. He doesn't need to come in here and be asking us questions; he's not my boss." In ministry it can sound like this, "I was praying for that person and she just came over and interrupted and started praying, too." Good leadership always establishes the need for boundaries and the concept of boundaries.

Remember that healthy boundaries have to be flexible. If they get too rigid, they are on the way to becoming walls. As Christians, if we are led by the Spirit it is much easier to know when we are supposed to do something and when we are not. No anointing is a good sign that you probably should have put up a boundary and said, "No," but you didn't. It's never too late to start and it will take some practice, but I promise you boundaries can change your life.

I encourage you to do two things. The first is to examine your own life. Do you tend to have difficulty setting boundaries or do you find yourself putting up walls? Are there some relationships you find easier to establish boundaries in than others? Why? Pray and ask the Holy Spirit for insight on why it is so difficult to establish boundaries. Second, if you have not read the book, *"Boundaries"* by Cloud and Townshend. I recommend that you purchase it and study it. If you've already read it, a second read never hurts.

Chapter 6
Self-Love and Care

Until we are able to come to genuine self-love, the rest of what I have written about is virtually impossible. I am not talking about narcissism, which is a dysfunctional self-love that is unable to empathize and truly love others. What I am talking about is an acceptance of how God made you, the ability to celebrate yourself, flaws and all and the ability to know that you are worthy of care. Unrequired martyr like behavior may look or feel noble at the time, but it is just self-destructive and stupid in the long run. God and others are really not requiring it. People who tend to martyr in an unhealthy way usually end up resentful and exhausted because there is no grace for it.

Take for example the mother who spends everything on her husband and children. Her wardrobe is in shambles, her hairstyle hasn't been updated in twenty years and her make-up drawer consists of samples from department stores. You get the picture. The children have the latest in fashion, her husband has every technological gadget he needs and she is still conducting conversations on a flip phone that is her daughter's hand me down. Why is everyone in the family more valuable than she is? Everyone has their own unique answer. But if you are martyring yourself in an unhealthy way, it's time to fess up and deal with the root issues. It's a trickledown effect. When you feel good about yourself, you are more comfortable being intimate with your spouse, which creates a stronger marriage. A stronger marriage leads to a healthy family and a healthy family will support you in your ministry or profession and be there for you when you need it.

Another sign of unhealthy martyr behavior is the ministry family who never takes vacations or time off. Everything revolves around ministry. Vacation looks like a trip to a city for a conference, three sessions a day, unless they go crazy and take a morning and afternoon off, maybe one trip to a theme park and everyone is supposed to be happy. They feel guilty whenever money or time is spent on something besides ministry. I know that being in the ministry does require sacrifice, but Jesus paid the ultimate sacrifice so we can have life and life more abundantly. Those kids are not mature enough and haven't made the decision to make that kind of sacrifice, but Mom and Dad make it for them. The children see their childhoods sacrificed on the altar of ministry and decide they don't want to have any part of a God who requires that. They move into rebellion and the parents are shocked because they brought them up in ministry. In the past, missionary organizations actually had homes on safe islands where all the missionary kids could be kept. They visited home a couple times a year. Can you imagine how they felt? I've ministered to some of the parents who are now dealing with the guilt and pain of what they lost then and what they are going through now because of estranged relationships. I've ministered to some of the children who were often abused by older children or even by workers in these missionary schools. What a horrendous practice! That would never happen with healthy priorities. Children need touch and healthy affection and, if they don't have it legitimately, they will find it illegitimately. That is why incest between siblings happens in homes where love is not demonstrated by physical touch and affection. I think martyring families is one of the worst sins the Church has committed. Okay, enough of my soap box, let's get back to you.

In Leviticus 19:18 it says, *"You shall not take vengeance, nor bear any grudge against the children of your people, but you shall love your neighbor as yourself."* If you don't treat yourself with love and respect, it's very difficult to treat others that way. I have found when ministering to others that if they can't forgive themselves they have a difficult time forgiving others. Sometimes it's good to stop and ask the questions, "Would I be doing that if I genuinely loved myself? Would I be thinking that if I genuinely loved myself? Would I be allowing that if I genuinely loved myself?" Adults who do not love themselves also carry a lot of anger toward others. Because they have not matured to be able to love and care for themselves, they are angry at everyone around them for not doing it for them. When we have the love of God in our lives and self-love and care, our demands on others become realistic. It becomes the whipped cream of our life, wonderful when we receive it, but not the substance.

The Bible tells us in 3 John 1:2 to pray that you may prosper even as your soul prospers. What is our soul? It is our mind, our will and our emotions. All of that needs to be prospering for us to truly prosper. Without self-love, it is impossible to truly prosper. People who remain in poverty have never really learned to love themselves. Here's what the process should look like. Our spirit is dead in sin until we are "born again." We become new creatures with a living spirit. Our spirit's job is to co-labor with the Holy Spirit to renew our minds, heal our broken hearts and restore and focus our will towards spiritual obedience. When they don't understand the process, people become disillusioned, disappointed and angry with God because everything in their life wasn't "all better"

42

when they got saved. It's important that we renew our minds to the love of God, knowing that He first loved us. Then we can begin to move into a revelation of self-love that begins the restorative process of God in our lives.

Self-love and care requires care in every area of our life. We might care for ourselves spiritually while physically we are being abusive to our bodies. I overworked my body for many years. One day I was in our ministry house pouring myself another cup of coffee to get ready for another counseling session. The Lord spoke to me as I was getting ready to take a sip. "If you continue to drink caffeine, I will not be able to give you a greater measure of my anointing." My mind immediately was like, "What are You talking about?" Here was His reply, "Caffeine quickens your body and my Spirit quickens your mortal body. It is the same Spirit that raised Christ from the dead. I know what your body can take, but you use caffeine as a whip to drive yourself further. Because I love you I will not put any more anointing on your life causing you to kill yourself prematurely. I know when to put my anointing upon you and when to lift it to allow rest and recovery." WOW! Stopped me in my tracks as I poured the coffee in the sink; I had been drinking coffee since I was a little girl and caffeinated sodas as an adult. Anointing or caffeine? For me, it wasn't a question.

I had amazing grace on withdrawals even though I definitely experienced some. I had to rely on natural energy and the anointing, which was sometimes a bit scary. It required taking better care of myself, so I did have more energy available. As I have trusted the Lord in this area, I can see His wisdom. Side benefits were migraine headaches decreased by a huge degree, along with anger and irritation. I never realized how much caffeine was contributing to my anger issues. Now I am healthier, happier and yes, the anointing increased on my life. Please hear my heart. I am not sharing this to be your Holy Spirit, this was a transaction between the Lord and myself. I am not sharing this to pass judgment on caffeine consumption. For some people who suffer from ADHD, caffeine can actually cause a calming and focusing affect in the brain. I realize that for my body it was like poison.

Caring for ourselves takes time, money and resources. We may be so busy ministering to others we don't stop and get ministry for ourselves. That takes time. All of our money goes to taking care of others, leaving our basic needs unmet. Whenever God gives us anything, we give it away. I remember one point in my life when someone gave me an item that was valuable. I immediately started thinking of where to sow it. Once again I was stopped in my tracks. God said, "I wanted you to have that and, if you keep giving every good gift away, I will stop having people sow into your life. You can still sow when I lead you to but for right now I want you to receive."

There are also the little things we do for ourselves, that special bubble bath, a weekend staycation where you give yourself permission to stay in your pajamas the whole time or taking a whole day off from phone, email or text. Unplugging electronically can definitely be refreshing. There are so many little things we can do - curl up with a good book, sleep in, ride a bike, go for a walk, dig in the dirt and plant some flowers – I could go on and on. Everybody has something that just makes them feel good and special. Give yourself permission to have more of those moments.

Guilt, condemnation and unworthiness are three of the biggest enemies of loving ourselves. Fact and experience may be that you were never loved, valued or appreciated as a child; but Truth declares that God loves you and now it's time to love yourself. A little self-love goes a long way in creating a life worth living. It's a great example for others and the example in a Godly, healthy way is so needed in the world. I think part of the reason we tend to shy away from it is because narcissism and selfishness is so ugly and repulsive - but true self-love is honoring to God. We are to be a reflection of Him in the earth. Hating, rejecting and neglecting ourselves do not bring Him glory.

Self-love and care can be reflected in our self-talk. How do you talk to yourself? Some of us talk to ourselves in tone and word in ways we would never speak to someone else. When you love yourself, you talk to yourself like someone you love. You don't beat yourself up. You don't keep a magnifying glass on your mistakes. You forgive yourself. Think about it. The next time you tell yourself, "You're fat. You'll never change. You're a loser," stop and think if you would say those things to someone else. Of course not. Your self-talk is a good indicator of how much you love yourself.

Evaluate: Where are you lacking in self-love and care? Why? What is the root to this ungodly fruit in your life? Ask the Holy Spirit, what are some things what would need to change for you to demonstrate self-love and care? Digest it a bit. As Christians we ingest all the time. Another word, another message, another scripture, another prophesy, another book, etc. But we need more digestion. When we don't have self-love we gulp our food and don't take time for digestion which is another one of my sins I am still working on in my own life. We can do the same thing in our spiritual life. We gulp another message and then it's over and gone with no thought, meditation, evaluation, study or activation. Just on to the next. Love yourself, slow down and digest.

Chapter 7
Rest

Burnout happens to us physically, mentally, emotionally and spiritually when we do not take time to rest. In our modern day Western Culture, we think a week's vacation once a year is rest. And normally that is crammed with a full itinerary of activities. We were created in God's image. He rested after the six days of creation and then He instituted the Sabbath as a way to teach us that we need rest, too.

I am old enough to remember when America still honored Sunday as a day of rest. Stores weren't open, people went to church and then spent time with their family and they rested. We were healthier as a society back then. I still love to go to Israel because there is still a large majority of people who recognize the Sabbath. It is like letting your spirit, soul and body take a deep breath and let it all out. The city of Jerusalem is quiet. Traffic ceases, the business of life quiets and people, families, cities and the whole country takes a deep breath. It's a wonderful time that starts with Shabbat dinner and then at the end of the Sabbath there is celebration as everyone returns to life.

My Story

Let me tell you my own story, because I am very busy, love productivity, and living and just doing. In the past, I tried to take days of rest but they could be easily overridden by something that needed to get done. In my late forties, I acquired mycoplasma bacteria that went undiagnosed for quite a while. I had traveled to a number of foreign countries and could have developed it there or at home. Mycoplasma bacteria can affect a number of areas in the body. Mine started with a bout of a very bad flu. I became extremely sick. It felt like I was dying but no one could tell me what was wrong. One of the things written about mycoplasma bacteria is that you will feel like you're dying because it sucks the cholesterol out of your cells and leaves you with no energy. I also became hyper sensitive to smells, chemicals and could barely make it out of my bedroom. When I did, I wore a mask. I was so sick, I couldn't read, watch TV or work on my computer. I was just left to lay and breath. My only solace was in the Lord. As it lingered on and I was not bouncing back like I would after a normal sickness, it began to get really

48

scary. I had been given a steroid early on and had an allergic reaction and ended up with a swollen spleen on top of everything. Enough said.

One day, I heard the Lord's voice. He said, "I've come for my Sabbaths." Suddenly I saw all those times I was too busy to rest. Please hear my heart. I don't think God gave me the condition. I gave me the condition by not taking care of my body the way I needed to in order to fight off the attack. But He uses everything and works it to our good. In my recovery, I could only eat organic. Anything that had chemicals in it affected me and I had no desire for it. I made some real commitments to the Lord at that time regarding the Sabbath rest and really taking care of my body. The mycoplasma bacteria was finally diagnosed and I began a very natural regiment to treat it. I didn't know if I would every redevelop my natural strength and energy. But praise the Lord; He created us with renewing power. I can say now in my sixties that I feel better and have more energy than I did in my forties. My energy has been so renewed that I took a 2,600-mile motorcycle ride from Florida to Montana with my sister and brother. When we arrived at his home, I still felt great.

I think we can also go so overboard on trying to do everything perfectly for our health that we can lose the joy of life and allow anything out of our normal regiment to cause stress and anxiety.

That's not healthy either. I still work at eating about eighty percent organic, but I can go out to eat with friends and enjoy myself. I may not have a perfect Sabbath rest because of a travel schedule, but I can take a little longer and I can Shabbat inside. I have learned the Lord is not a driver. We drive ourselves. I have accomplished more in the years where rest has become a priority than I ever did when I was trying to get so much done. Now when I look back I can laugh at how ridiculous I must have looked to the Lord.

Most studies you read related to cultures that have high rates of longevity and centurions in their population will all tell you that those societies have a couple things in common. Rest and social interaction are two important common variables. They rank higher than diet or exercise. Most of their exercise comes from their natural work and environment rather than a gym membership. They are cultures where napping and resting are ingrained into their everyday life and not reserved for a sick day or a mental collapse.

The Lord healed on the Sabbath and ministered on the Sabbath, but He still took time to draw away from the crowds to rest. I think we can acquire a healthy attitude towards natural rest without getting into religious bondage over it. As pastors, we took Monday as our Sabbath because Sunday was a work day. It's your job to get your own revelation and strategy. I can't tell you, "This is how you have to do it." I can only share my own story and testimony.

Enter His Rest

We will never be able to enter into natural rest until we first enter into spiritual rest.

Therefore, since a promise remains of entering His rest, let us fear lest any of you seem to have come short of it. For indeed the gospel was preached to us as well as to them; but the word which they heard did not profit them, not being mixed with faith in those who heard it.

For we who have believed do enter that rest, as He has said: "So I swore in My wrath, 'They shall not enter My rest,' " although the works were finished from the foundation of the world. For He has spoken in a certain place of the seventh day in this way: "And God rested on the seventh day from all His works (Hebrews 4:1 - 4:4 NKJV)

When we believe the Word of God and mix faith with it, we enter into spiritual rest. His Promises become "Yea and Amen" in our life. God said it; I believe it. But sometimes that's much easier said than done. Our circumstances often scream out something very different, just like they did for the children of Israel when they were wandering around the wilderness with enemies trying to kill them. It sure didn't look like God had a land for them. Sometimes we may have rest in one area of our life but not in another. Maybe we can rest knowing God has our children, but our finances still cause stress and worry. Or we may be in a place of faith and rest related to provision but not with our health. Sometimes rest is achieved in stages and progression as we truly mix our faith with the Word of God. But every area we conquer means more spiritual rest.

There remains therefore a rest for the people of God. For he who has entered His rest has himself also ceased from his works as God did from His (Hebrews 4:9 - 4:10 NKJV)

A Better Me

It's hard to enter into natural rest when you are not in spiritual rest. It makes you want to try a little harder, work a little longer and you end up believing if you push yourself and accomplish enough, God will be pleased with you. God is pleased with obedience. He is just as happy if I am taking a nap on a day of rest as He is when I am counseling, ministering, working, etc.

Let me tell you, it took me a long time to get here. For some personalities, it's an easier process than for others. I could have easily said, "That's just the way I am, I like to stay busy and productive." But that cop-out just doesn't work with God, especially when the main mission is for us to be transformed into the image of Jesus Christ.

My dad's favorite expression from Northern Minnesota was, "Its daylight in the swamp, time to get up and go to work." Our family was raised with a strong work ethic. A lot of it was good and I am so thankful for it; but when I felt guilty for resting in the middle of the day or couldn't rest unless I was sick, that portion had to be rooted out. A lot of illness comes from people's body giving them the excuse they need to rest. I had to work on developing beliefs that helped me renew my mind in this area. For example, "Rest is healthy for me spiritually, emotionally, mentally and physically and improves my relationships with the Lord, my family and others. I am a better me when I rest." Another one is "True productivity comes from the Lord. His favor, ability to multiply and create divine appointments is what I need to accomplish all He has for me." You get the idea. I needed specific mind renewal in this area. When we get fresh revelation and understanding, it's much easier to implement the Word of God. When we are rested, we are stronger physically and spiritually. Our discernment is keener and we are more aware of the enemy. Our ability to fight off temptation is greater. Even in little things - I can resist those cookies rested but tired, I am cramming one too many in my mouth.

What do you need to be a better you? If you think it's adding one more thing to your plate, it's probably not. Actually, it's more like, "What do I need to take off my plate so that I have the time to rest physically and time in the Word so I can truly enter His spiritual rest?" Ask the Holy Spirit to show you. Usually in His infinite wisdom, it's incremental changes. Sometimes we try to change too much too fast through will power. We end up defeated and frustrated. It's best to be guided by the wisdom of the Holy Spirit when bringing change to our lives.

Performance Defeated

Rest is critical for humility. It humbles us. It reminds us of God's bigness and His abilities. It's the best antidote for pride and performance. When we think that it's our work and our ability that greases the wheels of the Kingdom, God will show us that He can birth a nation in a day. He can bring deliverance and healing in a moment. He can give us one idea more profitable than years of work. I hate to tell you but at the core of our inability to rest is the fact that we don't really trust God. The Israelites didn't trust God to fulfill His Promise.

It's pretty hard to trust something you can't see. Yet in our daily lives we trust gravity, electricity, digital communication, etc. Stuff happens all the time that we can't see but we have learned to trust. It is possible. We begin to trust those things by interacting with them. It's the same way with God. He says that it's okay to actually test Him in different aspects. We can find a good example in Malachi 3:10 *"Bring all the tithes into the storehouse, That there may be food in My house, And try Me now in this,"* Says the LORD of hosts, *"If I will not open for you the windows of heaven and pour out for you such blessing that there will not be room enough to receive it."*

He offers us a challenge. Try His Word and see if He is not real. Trying God in this one aspect of provision can make a difference in how you rest in relationship to your finances. I remember the first time I tested God related to tithing as a brand new believer. When I gave my tithe the first Sunday, I knew I wouldn't have enough gas money for the week but I was determined to test God and see if He was real. On Tuesday of that week, a gentleman who had owed me money for a number of months (I had actually written it off) came to me with the amount in hand. I was impressed. I have been a tither ever since.

In today's language trusting the unseen would be, "Hook up this router in your house and suddenly you will be able to connect to websites around the world." But you have to do it to find out, "Yes, I can trust my router to give me a signal and provide me with information from around the world." Our spiritual router is the Holy Spirit. He is our hook-up here on earth and He brings the reality of a God we can trust in our everyday lives.

John 14:16 - 14:17 *"And I will pray the Father, and He will give you another Helper, that He may abide with you forever – "the Spirit of truth, whom the world cannot receive, because it neither sees Him nor knows Him; but you know Him, for He dwells with you and will be in you."*

I encourage you to try God in the area of rest spiritually and naturally. See what happens after really seeking the Holy Spirit on how you can enter into His Rest.

Chapter 8
Health and Longevity

The proceeding chapter is the foundation we first have to lay in our life before we can talk about health and longevity. Without it, anything else that's discussed is doomed to fail. Without a balance of rest in our lives, which also includes good sleep, we have stress and crave all the wrong foods. Rest creates positive chemical balances in our mind that are important in alleviating unhealthy desires. Without rest, we don't have the energy or desire for activity or exercise. I am not going to go into great depth here, but take time to study the effects of cortisol on the body. Cortisol is a hormone produced by stress and it causes weight gain, food cravings and other health problems. And it's not the only thing that can become unbalanced when we don't have proper rest.

Embracing Life

The first thing that has to happen related to health and longevity is that we have to embrace life. For years I was angry that I was even here. I didn't like life. Even after I was saved I was ready to make the trip to heaven ASAP. That was because I hadn't learned how to really live. Once you learn how to really live you will want to have as many years on this earth as you can. And you can embrace all of it, the ups and downs, the joys and sorrows of life. You can learn to be excited about living even when it's not always going the way you like it. Now I want to do everything in my power to stay healthy and live a long, full life and go home because God has deemed it's time and not because disease has taken my life. We have to learn how to receive healing so we are not walking around wounded and in emotional pain. And discovering our purpose is important, as well. What are your gifts; why are you here on earth? Those are important questions. Mark Twain said, "The two most important days in your life are the day you are born and the day you find out why." As we begin to serve God and others, we find out why we are really here. Also, when our relationships heal we want more time to be with our loved ones and be involved with our grandchildren's and great grandchildren's lives. On most Sundays at church we have four generations worshipping together. It excites me to think about worshipping with my great grandchildren when they arrive and being an example and demonstration to them. When we are wounded, our relationships are damaged and we don't really have purpose. Life equals pain. Everyone with any sense wants to escape pain. Isaiah 61 tells us all the good stuff Jesus came to do in our life. It's the Gospel, the Good News, prophesied of in the Old Testament. Read it. Meditate on it. If God did all those things for you, wouldn't you want to live? I have tested those Scriptures, first in my own life and then in the lives of many others. He really does want to heal our broken hearts, set us free, give us double honor for shame and all the other wonderful things that chapter shares.

When you truly embrace life, your health and well-being take on new meaning. Your days on earth become precious. Your lifestyle choices will begin to reflect the degree to which you value life. That's why so many people after they have a wake-up call like a heart attack or cancer make significant lifestyle changes. Is it just because the doctor said? No, it's the fact that their life was almost taken and now they have put a new value on it. One of my favorite scriptures is Psalm 68:19 *"Blessed be the Lord, Who daily loads us with benefits, the God of our Salvation! Selah."* Once we begin to receive His Benefit Package our lives become worth living. There are a lot of people showing up at jobs every day motivated by their desire for the benefit package. None of those can hold a candle to His

Benefit Package. It will help you show up to life every day.

Nutrition

There are so many studies, opinions and new revelations on nutrition. My job is not to educate you on all that; it's simply to say that nutrition is an important element of health and longevity. If I had a car that wouldn't run and I blew up the motor prematurely because I tried to run sugar water in it, I wouldn't get a lot of sympathy or prayer. I know I wouldn't want to lay hands every day on that car trying to believe for a miracle so that it would run. I would rather lay hands on the owner to get wisdom on how to take care of their car.

Yes, there are miracles of healing and I am thankful for that but we also have to understand that our bodies are created with innate, divine healing mechanisms within them. Systems to protect from germs and bacteria are part of our body's daily function. Wounds that can heal and organs that can regenerate are all part of the wonderful way we were created. The body is complex and designed to function by eating the food God created. Everything you will ever read on health, nutrition and healing of the body will always come back to vegetables, fruits, nuts, grains and protein. They were all created by God. How much and in what combinations may be subject to question, but those are the basic building blocks. The more naturally we eat, the more naturally healthy we become. It's a war to get our taste buds wanting the right stuff, but it's a war that can be won -- and then desiring the right stuff becomes easy.

Thank God I was raised on fresh garden vegetables, locally raised beef, venison, fish we caught ourselves and wild berries we picked. Treats were just that, something special. Sneaking fresh green peas out of the garden was satisfying to us or picking handfuls of fresh wild raspberries or strawberries. In busy seasons of my life, I have grabbed fast food at times, but on any given occasion my first choice would have been a good home cooked meal. Why? That's how my taste buds were set as a child. Now, we have people who turn up their noses at real food because they prefer hamburgers and French fries or something that is handed out of a fast food window. Why? Because that's how their taste buds were set as children. When we truly believe that our bodies are the temple of the Holy Spirit, we start taking care of them like they were something special. My diet has improved over the years as my desire to live has increased. Things that weren't good for me began to fall off as the Lord convicted and brought revelation. Soda drinking is a thing of the past. I have been off caffeine for nearly twenty years, and at one time I was a serious coffee drinker. This season I've been really tackling sugar, which is one of the leading causes of inflammation in our bodies. Again, let the Holy Spirit show you where to start. What do you need to add and what do you need to get rid of in order to live healthier. Spend less time in the interior aisles of the grocery store and more time in the outer aisles, because that's where the fresh food is. You can't change your diet until you change your shopping cart and your refrigerator and your pantry.

Exercise

People can have differences in how they get their exercise. Some may love the gym, some enjoy sports, some like to run and others may prefer physical work. How you get your exercise is not the important aspect. What is important is that your body was designed for regular exercise. Without exercise we lose muscle, chemicals that are important for well-being are not released in our brain, we become stiff, we gain weight -- and that's just for starters. Our bodies were created for exercise. The more our society has become sedentary at work and at home the unhealthier we have become.

Now we can add play to that list. When I was young, the only times we weren't moving were when we were sick or in trouble. Children are now tethered to electronic devices, moving only their eyes and their fingers. What they see has movement, but they don't. If our generation has health problems, what will the next generation suffer from if we don't leave a good example? I hope one day I will have a grandchild say, "Can you believe you used to eat food that was full of different chemicals?" Right now it would be hard for one of my grandchildren to imagine riding in a car with both of their parents smoking like mine did, and telling them that people actually used to smoke on airplanes would be mind boggling. Times do change; it's our job to help them change for the best.

Without exercise we age prematurely. A good example of how this works is the disease osteoporosis. It affects bone density and without weight bearing exercise a person can easily develop this debilitating condition. This causes bones to become porous and easily fractured and affects the quality of life. It's proven that exercise helps decrease symptoms of depression. Our physical, mental and emotional health are all affected by exercise. Like nutrition, we have to accept that exercise is important for "staying fresh." Our job is to figure out what works for us.

I personally, enjoy the outdoors. I will use a gym when traveling or when the weather is bad, but my husband and I participate in an outdoor exercise boot camp. It works for us; the routine is always different and it gives us a combination of stretching, strengthening and cardio. We also like exercising through activities like bicycling, motorcycling and playing with our grandchildren. Some people love the gym atmosphere, others like a private workout at home. Find what works for you and keep enough variety in it so that you stick with it. Exercise and physical activity are main keys to health and longevity.

Spiritual Keys

The Bible also gives us spiritual keys for health and longevity. The commandment of honoring our mothers and fathers comes with the promise that life will go well and we will have long life. Proverbs 14:30 tells us that a sound heart is life to the body but envy is rottenness to the bones. Our physical health is affected by our emotional health. If our emotional health is not governed by spiritual principles, we will allow emotions like unforgiveness, bitterness, anger, etc. to take root in our lives. All of those unhealthy emotions will eventually affect us physically. We hear stories about people dying from a broken heart. We can't separate our emotional well-being from our physical health. And even more importantly, we have to develop a strong spirit with a good Biblical foundation in order to walk in the righteousness, peace and joy the Kingdom of God promises us.

We need to be Kingdom people. Even though

we are in this world, we are still not to become of this world. Our job is to keep our residency in the Kingdom and be ambassadors to the world. That perspective makes a difference in how we handle everything. I remember being amazed at some older Christians when I was first saved. They had such a grace and peace about them. No matter what was going on around them, their ship floated on calm seas. They had learned of the Rest of God and their faith had developed to a place where they trusted Him regardless of the circumstances. Stress is such a huge factor in our health and longevity. As the world gets busier and busier and life becomes more complex, you have to decide what's going to float your boat – the storms of life or Kingdom Seas. Personally, I got tired of getting seasick!

I encourage you to really study the Word of God related to health and longevity. I just shared a few scriptures here, but there is so much more to discover. God has an opinion about our physical health and has weighed in on it. He is concerned about us inside and out, the seen and the unseen. It's always best to head back to the manufacturer for the directions. He designed us and knows how His design works best. Get a vision for your future – Premature death? Early Alzheimer's disease? Poor quality of life? Or will it be a long and healthy life?

Chapter 9
Joy, Play, Fun, Laughter

You'll know you're dealing with a religious spirit if the very title of this chapter bothers you just a bit. We can sometimes get so serious about ministry and helping others that we lose our joy. It's like parents who get so focused on their kids' behaviors and performance that they stop having fun with them. This is a recipe for disaster. So many of us become "Marthas" who are so busy focusing on the work of the ministry that we lose touch with the Lord of the ministry. We've already discussed what performance does to us. But I can guarantee it's like a sponge that will quickly soak up any joy, fun, play or laughter in our lives.

Our God is the God of the Party. Look at all the Feasts and times of special celebrations the Israelites celebrated throughout the year. And what did the Prodigal's father do when he arrived home? He threw a party! He's the God who wants us to dance and sing and play instruments to celebrate Him. When the devil can take joy, play, fun and laughter out of our lives, he wins.

When's the last time you did something playful? Laughed till it hurt? Just did something for pure fun? If you can't remember, it's time to give yourself permission to enjoy life. I love my grandkids for many reasons, but I especially love how they can take a busy grandmother with all kinds of problems to solve and things to do and transform her into someone splashing in a pool or trying to decide if we should color the flower pink or purple. There are some people who don't have play in their life because they never really learned to play as children. It could be because of abuse and trauma, the effects of poverty and neglect, or way too much responsibility. There are many reasons, but I encourage you to examine this area and reclaim it.

The joy of the Lord is our strength. Nehemiah shared that spiritual insight with us. And he was leading a bunch of people who were both working and warring; they needed to know how to keep strong. The Lord's joy is something way beyond circumstantial happiness. I remember a day years ago when I was walking to get the mail on a beautiful, bird singing, blue sky, sun shining Florida day, I was singing and praising the Lord. All was well and I thought I was full of joy. As I opened the mailbox and pulled out an unexpected bill, I felt that sense of happiness running out of me. As I walked back to our house, the Lord spoke to me. He said, "You thought you had the joy of the Lord, didn't you?" I nodded silently. He said, "You had the joy of the day, my joy doesn't leave that quick. I want you to study my joy." I began a serious Bible study on joy -- what it is, where it comes from and what it does for us. I learned so much. Joy should be our foundation, a place from which we live, not a place we visit occasionally. It's a measure of our faith, our trust and how much we are able to feel God's love.

Enemies of Joy

Some of the enemies of joy are fear, anxiety, worry, strife, anger, jealousy, unforgiveness and bitterness. That's why the Lord admonishes us not to participate in those works of the flesh. They are the antithesis of joy. The lack of joy should immediately alert us that something is not right. We are not in the right relationship with love. When a child is loved or cared for, they are always returned to joy. One of the most important jobs a parent can do is to return their child to joy. I wish I had done a better job at that when my two girls were young. Because their minds hadn't been fully trained to get back to "joy camp," they turned to alcohol and drugs to try to get the job done. We literally create lifetime brain circuitry in children when we take them from a place of distress and return them to joy. Dirty diaper? No problem, we can get back to joy. Fall down-go-boom? No problem, we can get back to joy. Get in trouble-have a consequence? No problem, here's the path back to joy.

We have to renew our minds. Sometimes we just focus on the learning aspect of that, but I believe God **really** wants to renew our minds. When the trail back to "joy camp" has not been clearly marked, God wants to help us. But first we have to firmly believe that is where God really wants us to live. The Apostle Paul so aptly put it when he admonished us to count it all joy. No matter what the trials or tribulations, we are to stay in a place of joy, because Our Heavenly Father will work it to our good.

Sounds Like a Party to Me

It's sad to see when people who have a great sense of humor or the ability to have fun feel that they have to hide it when they come to the Lord. For too long, churches were tabernacles where they needed "No Partying Allowed" signs. They were quiet, reverent places, devoid of any sense of joy. A quick study of the Tabernacle of David demonstrates that God had a different plan in mind. David had the leaders of the Levites appoint singers and people who played different types of instruments. We are talking harps, trumpets, stringed instruments, cymbals. They were to raise their voice with resounding joy. As the Ark of God was coming into the city, David was whirling and playing music. That was when Michal, Saul's daughter, caught sight of him and despised him in her heart. David's Tabernacle was a place of twenty-four hour praise and worship. When they dedicated the tabernacle after bringing in the ark of God, they made offerings. Afterward, David distributed a loaf of bread, a piece of meat and a cake of raisins to every man and woman. Sounds like a party to me.

Health Benefits of Laughter

The book of Proverbs was given to us so that we could learn wisdom. Proverbs 17:22 says, *"A merry heart does good, like medicine, But a broken spirit dries the bones."* Medical science now concurs with the Word of God; laughter is good for your health. Here are a few of the health benefits of laughter:

- Laughter boosts the immune system by decreasing stress hormones and increasing immune cells along with infection-fighting antibodies.
- Laughter relaxes our body and relieves physical tension. A real good laugh can leave your muscles relaxed for up to 45 minutes.

- Laughter causes the release of endorphins in our brain. Those are the feel-good chemicals that we need for a sense of well-being.
- Laughter can temporarily relieve pain because of those same endorphins.
- Laughter protects the heart by improving blood flow and the function of blood vessels. It can decrease the chances of a heart attack and other cardiovascular problems by lowering blood pressure.
- Laughter stimulates other organs, for example, the lungs.
- Laughter can dissolve negative emotions such as anger, fear or sadness.
- Laughter can help us shift perspective, which is good for our mental health.

Wow, all those amazing benefits, and they're free! Plus, it's our choice. I think it's time to get intentional about laughter. Just think - it is always at our disposal and it feels good. The worst side effects could be the occasional sore cheeks or ab muscles, which will dissipate with regular use.

We need to learn to laugh at ourselves and not take everything so seriously. Do you even know what makes you laugh anymore? Who in your life makes you laugh? Take a laugh inventory. You might be someone who's never laughed much – it's not too late to learn. Practice, loosen up a little.

Find some good clean Christian comedians and order their DVDs or watch them online. You can even set laughter goals. Be determined to start with a minimum of one good laugh every day. If you're married, work on making each other laugh. If you're single, sow some laughter into family and friends.

I believe in holy laughter, as well. What do I mean by that? The Word talks about the Lord filling our mouth with laughter. There are times when my husband and I will be overcome with laughter in our own home. You can feel the anointing and it's something that you can't just control and stop. These have always been times when we've been going through things and need breakthrough and strength. I love those moments of holy laughter. They draw us closer to each other and to the Lord.

I don't think our Heavenly Father takes pleasure in how serious we are, how little time for joy we have or how miserable we are sacrificing everything for Him. That's dysfunctional fathering. There are times that require us to be serious and times that we need to process the pain of life, but when we find our buoyancy in joy those times won't pull us under. In the counseling room I have seen people move through the depths of pain and trauma only to find relief, joy and laughter on the other side of the process. Joy, play, fun and laughter all work together for your good. They aren't just a luxury; they are elements of life that are critical to your well-being. If you want to stay fresh in whatever you do, this fabulous four are like essential nutrients.

Chapter 10
Vision, Growth and Change

Vision is an energizing source. When people are not plugged in to vision, the Bible says that they perish. There are several levels to vision. We first have to plug in to the vision of the Kingdom of God. The next level is to plug in to corporate vision and then we need to have personal vision within the bigger picture. Sometimes people try to just find and live their personal vision outside of the larger context of vision. Usually, it will not produce the results they are trying to achieve.

When we connect to heavenly vision it creates divine energy. In Daniel 11:32b, it says, *"but the people who know their God shall be strong, and carry out great exploits."* That takes energy and it also takes transformation. Over and over again, we find people in the Bible who found strength, energy and abilities as they fulfilled their part of corporate vision.

Esther is a great example of someone who

found personal destiny by first plugging into corporate vision. Mordecai challenged her that she had to have a vision for the salvation of her people. When she plugged in to that and made her famous proclamation of *"If I perish, I perish,"* the greater vision caused her to become a woman ready to lay down her own life for her people. Her personal vision was also fulfilled because she found favor with the King and she became a famous queen who is still celebrated every year during Purim.

I'm here to tell you, it's impossible to stay fresh without vision. I'm not talking about dreams or wishes; I'm talking about the real thing. I encourage you to really study the Word related to the Kingdom of God so that you understand that you are a part of a much bigger vision. It will help you keep things in perspective. It will also help you not to personalize the reactions of others. When we over personalize, we get upset and emotionally worked up about other people's issues and reactions. This wears us out. We get all worked up over things the Bible tells us will happen because of the Kingdom of God. Persecution is a good example. It goes with the Kingdom.

Then within the vision of the Kingdom we need to be plugged into the corporate vision of church, ministry or helping organization. It also helps to create energy. As a pastor, I watched it happen over and over again. When people were plugged into the vision of the church, they were involved, energetic, enthusiastic and moving forward. If they became offended or hurt and pulled out of the vision, you could literally watch them wilt before your eyes. If you don't agree with the vision, you create di-vision which benefits no one.

Finally, you have to have your personal vision for what God has called you to be and do. What is your life supposed to look like? I believe Joseph's personal vision of being a leader caused him to rise to the top of every experience he had. Vision kept him from giving up in the prison and caused him to serve where ever he found himself.

The Bible also tells us to write the vision and make it plain. I encourage you write your own personal vision. There is something that happens when we establish our vision in writing. It may change and mature some as you go and that's okay. Just make sure it's not just your own vision for your life. The Word tells us that many are the plans of a man's heart but He orders our steps. Guard against personal ambition and pride and seek Him for a vision that will energize you and be a guiding force.

Pursuing Growth

There's a Southern saying that says, "When you're green, you're growing. When you're ripe you're rotting." It's always best to keep learning and growing. People who get ripe usually have a rotten attitude. They know everything, have done everything and they aren't a whole lot of fun to be around.

Continuing education and ministry is critical to staying fresh. We have to be receivers as well as givers. When we know it all we are ready for a fall. If a pastor is always preaching and never sits under the Word themselves, they are at risk of burnout. If the counselor is always pouring out but never confides in anyone else or is vulnerable related to their issues, it's a recipe for trouble. Whenever we feel like we have arrived, we are setting ourselves up for trouble. Humility is a key to keeping a heart attitude where you are always ready to learn and hungry to receive.

There are so many different ways we can continue learning and growing. We can do it through relationships, courses, classes, seminars, life experiences, books and the internet. I like to regularly pursue things I want to learn about and will buy books on the subject and study online articles. It's amazing how much information comes to you once you start focusing in a certain direction. I can thank so many of the people that I have worked with, because many times their issues required me to do a great deal of a study that still continues today. I've spent years studying sexual issues, eating disorders, addictions, dissociative identity disorder and a whole host of topics. Without learning, I would have not been as effective and I would have felt frustrated and defeated, which contributes to burn out.

One of the best ways of learning is spending time with the Lord. After all, He is the spirit of wisdom, knowledge, understanding and counsel. We can learn from revelation in the Word and through getting a God perspective on things. I enjoy the times I learn from intimate sharing in prayer when the Lord speaks to me in that still, small voice. The things He shares are life changing. We are supposed to be going from glory to glory or faith to faith, and if we aren't we won't stay fresh.

When we get stale our service to others gets stale and that's no fun for them or us. When we have a heart to learn, we will stay creative. Creativity is another God form of energy. Just like vision is an energizing force so is creativity. I promise you a creative day over another "in my rut day" will give you more energy, which leads us to the topic of embracing change because creativity requires change.

Embracing Change

I used to like the saying, "Blessed are the flexible because they won't break," but I've gone a step further in this season of my life. Now I would say, "Blessed are the fluid because they can be poured out." When you're fluid the Lord can pour you into any situation and you are able to flow.

When you're flexible, you're still in control trying to go along with things. When you're fluid, you've moved to a greater trust in the Lord and you just flow. The Holy Spirit isn't flexible. The Holy Spirit flows. The Bible says that we are sons of God when we are led by the Spirit. If He flows, He is going to want us to flow. We start off trying to control our lives, and then we realize it's going to take flexibility. But when we finally surrender to flow, that's when we find the real freedom.

Resisting change actually takes excess emotional energy. Change has happened whether you try to resist it or not. You can keep wearing your swimsuit in October but the bottom line is the season has changed. That's a pretty clear example of how important it is to accept change in a timely fashion. Hello, its fall – time to put a jacket on! That may be an exaggeration, but I am sure we have all had times in our lives where we were not ready to change with the new season. We hang onto relationships that have reached their expiration date and now they're stinky. We stay committed to old technology until we have frustrated everyone around us. We even say things about ourselves like, "That's just the way I am," which is one of the most self-defeating statements you can make. It's important to get to any painful roots related to change. As a child you may have had to face the change of moving a lot, resulting in social isolation, or the change of divorce, when your whole home life changed and left you feeling abandoned and lost. Let the Lord minister to those areas of painful change so you can embrace Kingdom change. Let's face it, it's impossible to stay fresh without change.

Some personalities embrace change easier than others, but we all need to realize that change is good. Change is healthy. Change can even be fun. We need to learn how to be proactive with change. I do an inventory every so often to see what's bothering me or even causing irritation in my life that can be changed. Sometimes it's a simple new purchase that will smooth out the rough edges of life. Like the perfect organizer in a cupboard drawer or some fluffy new towels. I look at what I can change and require change, and then I will throw in some change just to spice life up a little bit. Sometimes it's freshening up your home or work environment. Sometimes you have to freshen you. A new haircut, a new pair of glasses, some changes to your wardrobe -- whatever it is you will find change good for you and the people around you.

The Bible tells us that we are to be transformed in the very image of Jesus Christ. I don't know about you, but in my life that has taken a lot of change and I am not even close yet. In the previous paragraph I talked about some superficial changes. But even more important are those deep-down character and heart changes that we all need. When we resist those changes, we end up resisting the Lord. A wrestling match with Him never goes well on the side of humanity. Surrendering quickly to the changes He wants to make in us causes life to go much better for us. Run towards the change, not away from it.

Vision, growth and change are all critical elements to keeping a fresh attitude toward life and service. I know many of the things I've shared in this book aren't new. But I hope by sharing them you will be reminded of how important you are and how necessary it is for you to take care of yourself. In Matthew 9:17 Jesus gave a parable about the importance of using new wineskins because old wineskins get dry and brittle and bust open. New wineskins are soft and supple and able to expand. We need to continue to be those new wineskins, trusting that He will keep us filled with the new wine of anointing, so that we can be poured out into the lives of others.

In Summary

I said in the dedication to *Staying Fresh* that as ministers, teachers, counselors and caregivers you are builders of the future. You help, support and educate the people of our future. You are important and if you want to stay in the game of helping others, your longevity and effectiveness will depend on how well you implement what's been shared in *Staying Fresh*. Hanging in, bitter and burnt out, doesn't count. I'm talking about being someone who can stay in the business of serving others and remain fresh, with your joy, your health, your family, your spirituality and your overall well-being intact.

It's not about doing everything perfectly every day, but it is about living intentionally. And if you get off course, now you have a road map. This is one of those books that a quick review every six months can help you quickly make a course adjustment. I live by these principles, but in writing the book I have been challenged to do better. My hope and prayer for you is that if you have been in burnout this book will help you know what to do differently when you get back in the game again. But more importantly, I pray that this book reaches you before you ever come to that point.

I shared that in my early twenties I received advice that has stayed with me. The advice was to take care of myself and my family if I wanted to help others long term. I have always tried to pass this counsel on to others. This time I did it through authoring *Staying Fresh*. I encourage you to pass it on, too. Please share a copy with someone and let's keep our life helpers healthy and fresh.

RECOMMENDED RESOURCES

Order by contacting: **info@KingdomLifeNow.com**

Restore My Soul – 90 Day Devotional
Soul Battles
Birth Assignments
A Woman's Guide To Freedom
The Prodigal Daughter – Novel
Redeemed – Novel

Made in the USA
Middletown, DE
30 April 2017